I0617307

THE SUNDAY SCHOOL ELEPHANT

By Rezwana Derbyshire as told by Doug Derbyshire

Illustrated by Jerry and Faith McCollough

Copyright © 2023 Rezwana Derbyshire and Doug Derbyshire
All rights reserved. No part of this book may be reproduced or used in any manner without the prior written permission of the copyright owners, except for the use of brief quotations in a book review.

To request permissions, contact the publisher at Admin@TellTheKids.com

Hardback ISBN: 978-1-953935-16-8
Paperback ISBN: 978-1-953935-17-5
Ebook ISBN: 978-1-953935-18-2

First edition February 2023

Author Rezwana Derbyshire
As told by Doug Derbyshire
Edited by Anna Derbyshire
Cover art by Jerry and Faith McCollough
Layout Design by Alissa Costello
Illustrations by Jerry and Faith McCollough

Printed by Ingram Spark in the USA
Published by
Tell The Kids®, LLC
Fort Worth, TX

TellTheKids.com

To our children and our children's children
for generations to come.

On a beautiful day in a land far away,

Many Sundays like this there have been,

The people of God in a quaint little town

Sat waiting for church to begin.

Dr. Doug and his daughter gathered the kids

And they sat 'neath a large Banyan tree,

Doc opened his Bible and smiled a big smile

"We're starting in Genesis 3."

Sin shattered the bond between man and God

As it barged into the world.

It tore apart the plans that God made

As around mankind it swirled.

Creation had turned
from good to wicked

**Sin threw it all
in the mud**

Though it broke God's
heart, He'd wipe the
earth clean

Through ruin, and
wreckage and flood.

Then out of nowhere
arrived an old friend

Intruding the Doc's
lesson plan,

With a mammoth in tow
and a big "Hello!"

Out walked
Mr. Elephant Man.

8

It had been many years since
he saw this big brute

Its memory he could
not dismiss,

God had used this big
bumbling gobbler of fruit

But it's temperament
was hit or miss.

Oh no! Not again! Was the thought in Doc's head

Faced once more with this meddlesome beast,

He knew what's in store, since he'd seen this before

He feared his teaching might cease.

Despite the presence of this pachyderm pet

The children were wholly unmoved

"What happened next?" They asked Dr. Doug

They wanted the Doc to resume.

"God chose the man Noah to survive those dark days

And told him to build a big boat,

God saw he was righteous - most blameless on earth

So, He chose to keep Noah afloat.

God gave him directions to build as He said:

'Use wood. Make it high and quite wide,

Use tar to keep the floodwaters out

Build three decks and a door on the side.

So, Noah began his work on the ark

No rain, no downpour in sight,

The people around him jeered and they laughed

They called him a liar outright.

Noah held onto the promise of God

And kept doing what God said to do,

He gathered his bride, his sons and their wives

And animals paired two by two.

God gave strict instruction to find and assemble

All creatures that lived in the land,

Even gnats and elephants boarded the ark

No creature too small or too grand.

Then the gargantuan creature disrupted the teacher

And punctured the air with his noise,

This big beast of burden seemed pretty certain

He could dazzle the girls and the boys.

Doctor Doug closed his Bible, and turned to his guests

Resigned to this unforeseen twist.

Doubtless the lesson was done for the day

Since an elephant is hard to resist.

The Doc expected the kids to jump up

And run to the beast they adore.

But none of them moved, not even a muscle

"Don't stop, we want to hear more!"

The Doc, surprised, reopened his Bible

He tried to suppress his expression,

With the elephant lurking behind their small class

He flipped back to Genesis seven.

Safe on the ark and sheltered from rain

They witnessed the flooding of earth,

For forty long days it thundered and stormed

As the world was rinsed and rebirthed.

Huddled onboard, they waited for days-

Some three hundred ten and five.

Noah, his bride, his sons and their wives

Were grateful God kept them alive.

When the rains came and poured on the earth

Noah's warnings were all proven true,

Obeying the Lord - no matter the cost

Was surely the right thing to do.

The elephant reared on its two back legs

Hopping and doing a dance.

But the children dismissed the mammoth at play

They barely gave it a glance.

The Doc snuck a glance at his unwelcome guest

Amazed, he asked himself "How?"

How could the kids turn their backs and their gaze

From this remarkable tusky cow?

The Doc was euphoric God's Word was their focus

He dove right back into the text.

It was important that since God was making the way

He tell the kids what happened next.

The moment was here, God said, "It's time

For the passengers to disembark."

They all ran out with joy no doubt

And life began outside the ark.

The elephant roared now louder than ever

Flapping its ears it pranced

But still the children paid it no mind

They didn't give it a chance.

An altar was built to honor the Lord

Noah worshiped with all of his might,

God was so pleased with the scent of their love

That he filled the sky with a sign.

God placed a rainbow high in the clouds

His resplendent promise unfurled

"Never again will floodwaters rise

To submerge and flood the whole world."

"Replenish the earth with life anew"

God said to all who remained

"The earth is restored, now sin no more

Love Me and honor My name."

Dr. Doug closed his Bible and looked at the kids

No peep, no sound could be heard.

They were stunned into reverent, awestruck silence

Overwhelmed by God's Holy Word.

God's Word was presented, Noah's story was told

Overcoming a mammoth distraction.

The elephant did its best to amaze and impress

But God's Word was the bigger attraction.

Walking home with his daughter, Doc marveled and pondered

His mind filling up with this thought,

Though the Doc's intention was to teach a good lesson

In the end it was him who was taught.

Our job is to teach God's Word with boldness

It's His job to make Himself known,

42

God doesn't need us to make His Word sparkle

He can do that all on His own.

Tell The Kids...

This is a true story of an elephant who came to Sunday School. It is also true when the Bible teaches us God flooded the earth and saved Noah with his family. The Bible also tells us that Jesus, God's son, came to earth to save the earth from sin. Dr. Doug Derbyshire and his wife Cheryl went to Thailand as missionaries to tell people, who have never heard they can be saved, that Jesus wants to save them and make them born again, just like the earth was born again after the flood.

To be born again, is to be washed clean of sin. Just like in the story of Noah, the sin on the earth needed to be washed away, so our hearts need to be washed and made clean in order to serve God.

If you want to have your heart washed clean and be Born-Again, you can pray right now:

Pray and tell God that you believe that He made the world.

Tell God that you believe He is holy and perfect and confess to Him that you are not.

Thank God for His love and thank Him that His Son Jesus came to wash away our sins by dying for us on the cross.

Ask Him to cleanse you of all your sins, and tell him your commitment to live to honor him from this day on.

Some of the children who were visited by an elephant in Sunday school that day gave their hearts to the Lord. Sandi grew up, got married, earned her nursing degree, and now serves the Lord with her husband. They all continue to tell people in Thailand and other countries how they can be born again.

Tell The KIDS.

www.ingramcontent.com/pod-product-compliance
Lightning Source LLC
Chambersburg PA
CBHW040818120626

46551CB00004B/587